Cumbria's Lost Railway

by

Peter W. Robinson

£3

Ex-LNWR 0-6-0, No. 28589, leaving Cockermouth Station with a service to Workington in the 1930s.

PICTURE ACKNOWLEDGEMENTS

The publishers wish to thank the following for contributing pictures to this book.

John Alsop for pages 9–11, 16, 18–21, 23, 26, 29–33, 37, 39, 40 (both), 42, 46 (upper), 48, the inside back cover and the back cover; the Cumbrian Railways Association for pages 1, 4, 8, 13, 14, 17, 22, 24, 27, 34–36, 38, 43–45, 46 (lower), and 47; Neville Stead for page 12; Neville Stead and B.G. Tweed for the front cover. The pictures on pages 15 and 41 are from the author's collection and the remaining pictures are from the publisher's collection.

Details of the Cumbrian Railways Association may be obtained from the Membership Secretary, 36 Cleveland Avenue, Barrow-in-Furness, LA13 0AE.

A train of the Furness Railway at Green Road Station, which is still open to services.

INTRODUCTION

Cumbria, as we know it today, was formed in 1974 from the former counties of Cumberland and Westmorland together with the Furness area of Lancashire and a small part of the West Riding of Yorkshire. It forms a fairly logical unit for the study of railway history – and one of fascinating variety as well.

The western half of Cumbria was dominated by railways of local origin, serving local industries which became of national importance with the early boom in steel manufacture in the 1860s and '70s. In the east were two north–south trunk routes linking England and Scotland, together with the cross-Pennine lines which were essential lifelines linking the industries of the Furness and West Cumberland areas with those of Tyneside and Teeside, as well as to the coalfields of Northumberland and Durham.

The county's present railway network comprises almost all the railways built before 1850, together with the famous Settle and Carlisle route, built in the 1870s, and the link across the south of the county between Carnforth and Ulverston which opened in 1857. The first railway in the county was the Newcastle and Carlisle which opened in stages between 1835 and 1838, being the successor to a proposal for a canal first mooted in 1796. The east–west rail route was then continued to the coast of the Solway Firth by the Maryport & Carlisle Railway which also opened in stages between 1840 and 1845. Over the following few years the route was completed round the coast by other local companies to link the local ports and their industries. The Furness Railway opened in 1846 to connect local iron ore mines and slate quarries to the coast for shipment. It soon grew extremely prosperous as local iron furnaces and other industries developed in and around the new town of Barrow which the railway company was actively involved in promoting and developing. The link eastwards from the Furness area, essential to support local industries and to export their products, was opened in 1857 by the Ulverstone and Lancaster Railway.

Inland from the coastal route in West Cumberland there developed one of the most intensive local rail networks seen in almost any part of the country. Tapping local resources of coal and iron ore, these locally owned lines paid massive dividends to their shareholders during the 1860s, but eventually they fell prey to takeovers by the London & North Western Railway and the Furness Railway. However, the new owners soon became complacent about the services they offered to local traders who turned to promoting their own railway to connect the Cleator ore field with the iron furnaces around Workington. Supporting the coastal industries, with supplies of Durham coke, were the cross-Pennine lines and the Cockermouth, Penrith and Keswick Railway, all built during the 1860s.

The first major trunk route was the Lancaster & Carlisle Railway, opened in 1846 as part of the completion of the West Coast main line to Scotland (this was continued north from Carlisle by the Caledonian Railway and opened two years later). The L&C became part of the LNWR from 1859. Within a few years it was being challenged by the Midland Railway as it sought to improve the handling of its traffic to and from Scotland. By 1875 the Settle and Carlisle line had become a reality after a long hard slog of five years of construction, though it was another year before it was open to passengers. Travel over this spectacular line was inaugurated by the introduction of new luxurious Pullman cars imported from America.

The arrival of the Midland Railway turned the railways of Carlisle into turmoil. New goods avoiding lines and a much enlarged station were built, the latter opening in 1880, all then to remain little changed for more than seventy-five years. The 'Border City', into which seven companies and eight lines ran, became very much the railway frontier between England and Scotland until the rapid rise and fall of Kingmoor Marshalling Yard in the 1960s and then electrification in 1974 removed much of Carlisle's key role.

The decline of Cumbria's railways began long before Beeching. As soon as deposits of coal or iron ore were exhausted, railways serving the mines closed. With the long term decline and demise of heavy industry in the coastal towns whole chunks of the network went as they became redundant, including the North Eastern lines which reached over Stainmore Summit to Penrith and Tebay. The 1980s saw the attempted closure of the Settle and Carlisle line by British Railways, but this was strongly fought by a consortium of local councils and supporters of the line. It survived the final ministerial decision of April 1989, having already seen the reopening of eight stations in 1986, with new passenger services; in the mid-1990s there was a revival of heavy freight traffic.

At the start of twenty-first century, the railways of Cumbria stand on the edge of a new era with an upgraded West Coast main line and much accelerated passenger services operated by the new Voyager and Pendolino trains. As such, this stands as an appropriate time to review the fascinating railway past of this beautiful county.

Annan (Shawhill) – Brayton Junction

Passenger service withdrawn	20 May 1921
Distance	15.5 miles
Company	Caledonian Railway

Stations closed	*Date*
Bowness *	20 May 1921

Stations closed	*Date*
Whitrigg *	20 May 1921
Abbey Junction *	20 May 1921
Bromfield *	20 May 1921

* Closed temporarily from 1 January 1917 to 2 March 1919.

Bowness Station, with a Caledonian Railway train approaching from the Solway Viaduct.

Ex-LNWR 0-6-0, No. 8414, at Abbey Junction Station, 25 June 1931.

The former Solway Junction Railway was planned as a cut-off route between Brayton on the Maryport & Carlisle Railway and the Caledonian Railway at Kirtlebridge. This would provide a shorter route than via Carlisle for West Cumberland hematite iron ore being carried in large quantities in the 1860s to the iron furnaces of Lanarkshire, and it would also enable this traffic to avoid the congested junctions at Carlisle. The line was opened for goods traffic on 13 September 1869 – passenger services began on 8 August the following year – on the promise that the cost of transporting ore into Scotland would fall by one shilling per ton. However, almost as soon as the line was completed the traffic evaporated as new blast furnaces were constructed in West Cumberland to smelt the ore locally. The Solway Junction Railway was soon in financial difficulties, compounded by the near destruction of the Solway Viaduct by ice flows in the Solway Firth in January 1881. The Scottish section of the line had already been transferred to the Caledonian Railway in 1873 and a complete merger with that company followed in 1895.

Abbey Junction Station, 25 June 1931. The ex-NBR line is on the left while the former Solway Junction line to Brayton Junction is on the right.

Bromfield Station, 25 June 1931.

The part of the line in England was separated into two sections, the three mile connection between Abbey and Kirkbride Junctions being provided by running powers over the Silloth branch of the North British Railway. After closure of the whole route in May 1921, the section between Brayton and Abbey was reopened, by agreement between the Caledonian and the Maryport & Carlisle Railway, to carry freight traffic from May 1922. It also continued as a link for the popular excursion traffic between West Cumberland and the small resort of Silloth, but was finally closed from 13 February 1933.

Alston – Haltwhistle

Passenger service withdrawn	3 May 1976	*Stations closed*	*Date*
Distance	Alston – County Boundary	Alston	3 May 1976
	at Gilderdale Viaduct: 1.5 miles		
Company	North Eastern Railway		

Alston Station, now the home of the South Tynedale Railway.

Promoted by the Newcastle & Carlisle Railway, with the support of the London Lead Company, to open up access to the lead mining area of South Tynedale, this branch opened on 1 January 1852 although the continuation to Nenthead was dropped from the final scheme. While the once extensive lead mining industry began to fall into serious decline from the 1870s, until closure the line continued to provide a lifeline to the outside world for Alston, the highest market town in England. The southern part of the branch has since been taken over by the South Tynedale Railway and is progressively being reopened as a 60cm narrow gauge line.

Arlecdon – Distington (Rowrah Branch Junction) *

Passenger service withdrawn Arlecdon – Oatlands: 1 January 1917
Oatlands – Distington: September 1922
Distance 6.75 miles
Company Cleator & Workington Junction Railway

Station closed   *Date*
Oatlands *   September 1922
Arlecdon *   1 January 1917

Oatlands Station.

'Baird's Line', the steeply-graded branch of the C&WJR from Distington to Rowrah, was opened on 1 May 1882 to link with the Rowrah & Kelton Fell Railway which had been opened in 1874 by the Scottish ironmasters William Baird & Co. to tap iron ore deposits in the remote fells of the western Lake District above Ennerdale. Later the branch was used to haul limestone from the quarries around Rowrah to supply the blast furnaces of Workington. The line survived until 8 August 1938 when the mineral traffic was diverted via Marron Junction (later it went via Moor Row; see also pages 31–32).

* Previously had a passenger service into Workington which ran from 3 July 1883 until July 1892. This service was reintroduced from November 1909 and extended to Arlecdon from 5 October 1912.

Arnside – Hincaster Junction

Passenger service withdrawn	4 May 1942	*Stations closed*	*Date*
Distance	5.25 miles	Sandside	4 May 1942
Company	Furness Railway	Heversham	4 May 1942

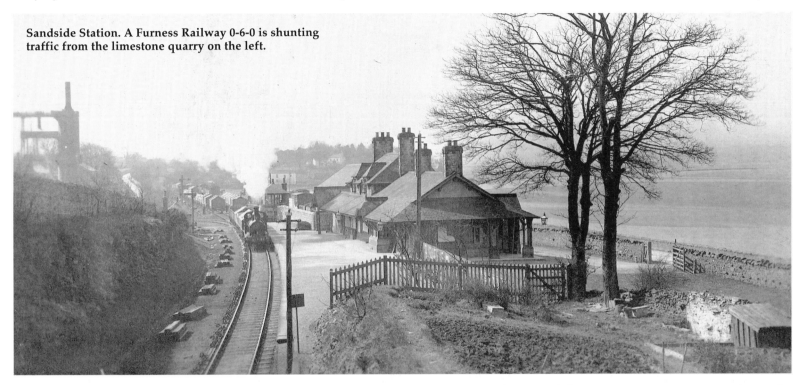

Sandside Station. A Furness Railway 0-6-0 is shunting traffic from the limestone quarry on the left.

From completion of the line across Stainmore (see pages 10–12 and 24) coke for the blast furnaces of the Furness area was transported over the Pennines, being transferred from the North Eastern Railway at Tebay onto the LNWR and then to the Furness Railway at Carnforth. This cut-off route was promoted to shorten the distance for the carriage of coke but, within a few years of opening on 26 June 1876, the traffic had reverted to its original route. This continued, with the line carrying only five trains a day between Kendal and Grange operated by the Furness Railway, until 2 September 1916. From that date, with railways under severe wartime pressure for operating economies, through workings between Tebay and the Furness area were resumed, their operation shared between the LNWR and the Furness Railway. Although passenger services were withdrawn from 4 May 1942, the coke traffic continued until the closure of Barrow Ironworks in 1962, the section north of Sandside then being closed from 9 September 1963. The remaining short line from Arnside continued to serve a large limestone quarry until 31 January 1971.

Barnard Castle (Tees Valley Junction) – Eden Valley Junction

Passenger service withdrawn	22 January 1962		*Stations closed*	*Date*
Distance Eden Valley Junction – County Boundary at Stainmore			Kirkby Thore	7 December 1953
	Summit: 20.5 miles		Appleby East	22 January 1962
Company	North Eastern Railway		Warcop *	22 January 1962
			Musgrave	3 November 1952
Station closed	*Date*		Kirkby Stephen East	22 January 1962
Clifton Moor	22 January 1922		Barras	22 January 1962
Clifburn	17 September 1956			
Temple Sowerby	7 December 1953		* Remained open for occasional military traffic until *c*.1983.	

Kirkby Thore Station.

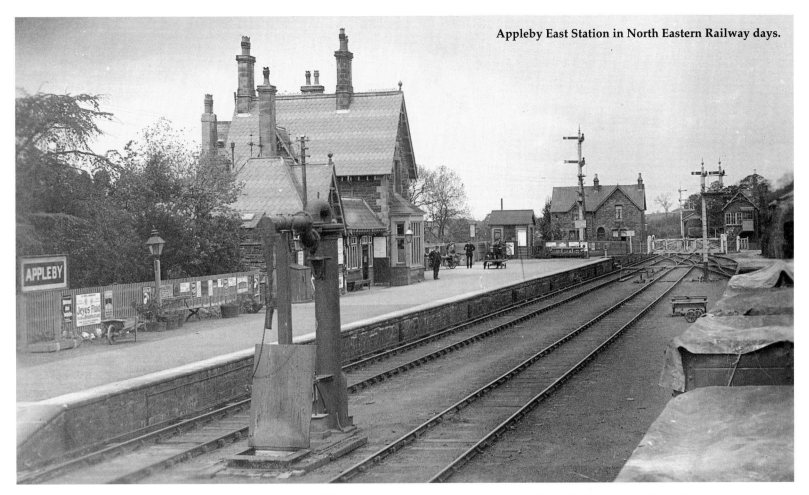

Promoted purely as a line of local significance, the Eden Valley Railway opened to passengers on 7 June 1862 between Kirkby Stephen and a south-facing junction at Clifton on the Lancaster & Carlisle Railway. With the promotion of the Cockermouth, Keswick & Penrith Railway, the Eden Valley provided part of a strategic link between the South Durham coalfield and the growing iron industry of West Cumberland. By 1 August 1863 a new north-facing curve was opened, which, with a detached section of the North Eastern Railway between Eamont Bridge Junction on the L&C and Redhills Junction, provided direct running onto the CK&PR. From the opening of that latter railway in 1865 until the mid-1920s, the Eden Valley line was to carry great quantities of coke to feed the blast furnaces of Workington.

BR 2-6-0s, Nos. 77003 and 76019, at Kirkby Stephen East, heading a final excursion from Darlington for enthusiasts on the last day of passenger services, 20 January 1962.

At its peak the section over Stainmore carried up to fifteen coke trains a day, some of them also bound for the iron furnaces of Furness, a traffic which continued until a year or two before final closure in 1962. Passenger traffic, however, was scant, with only four trains running between Darlington and Tebay before the grouping of railway companies in 1923. After 1923 the London & North Eastern Railway diverted through services to Penrith at the west end, but by 1960, a year before closure when diesel units were working the service, there were only three trains each way per day. Both the Eden Valley Railway and the South Durham and Lancashire Union Railway (between Barnard Castle and Tebay) were absorbed into the Stockton & Darlington Railway from 1 January 1863, and in turn into the North Eastern Railway. For notes on the line between Kirkby Stephen and Barnard Castle see the section for Kirkby Stephen East – Tebay on page 24.

Barrow Shipyard – Barrow (St Luke's Junction)/Barrow (Salthouse Junction)

Passenger service withdrawn	30 June 1967	*Station closed*	*Date*
Distance	1 mile	Barrow Shipyard *	30 June 1967
Company	Furness Railway		

* This station did not appear on public timetables. It was also known as Island Road Station.

With the expansion of the docks in Barrow in the 1870s the Furness Railway system was extended onto Barrow Island via opening bridges at the north end of Devonshire Dock and the south end of Buccleuch Dock. The growing shipyard on the island was taken over by Vickers in 1896 and the station at Island Road (later Shipyard) started from 1 May 1899 with worker's trains running from Millom and Grange. The station closed when the lifting bridge over the entrance to Buccleuch Dock was declared unsafe.

5MT 4-6-0, No. 45445, and 2-6-4T, No. 42376, await departure from Island Road Station with workmen's trains to Grange and Millom, 7 October 1960.

Barrow Ramsden Dock – Barrow (Shipyard Junction)

Passenger service withdrawn	April 1915	*Station closed*	*Date*
Distance	0.5 mile	Barrow Ramsden Dock	April 1915
Company	Furness Railway		

Included in the Furness Railway's plans for extension of Barrow's docks was the development of a deep-water pier for packet services to the Isle of Man and Belfast. A line was opened to Ramsden Dock Station on Barrow Island from 1 June 1881 and steamer services switched from the pier at Piel, south of Barrow, on the same day. Boat trains were operated from Leeds by the Midland Railway until the latter company completed the development of its own port at Heysham, with services transferring there from 1 September 1904. However, the FR continued to operate its own vessels on cross-bay services until after the outbreak of war in August 1914.

Brampton Town – Brampton Junction

Passenger service withdrawn	29 October 1923		*Stations closed*	*Date*
Distance	1 mile		Brampton Town *	29 October 1923
Company	Brampton Railway/North Eastern Railway			

* Previously closed from 1 May 1890 until 1 August 1913, and temporarily closed from 1 March 1917 to 1 March 1920.

From as early as 1798 a wagonway had linked Brampton with the collieries around Tindale which belonged to the Earl of Carlisle. This was rebuilt to make a junction near Milton in the 1830s when construction of the Newcastle & Carlisle Railway was in progress and reopened on 8 July 1835. A horse-drawn passenger service started soon afterwards, converting to steam operation in 1 July 1881. However, it was closed after an inspection by the Board of Trade in 1890. It was not until 1 August 1913 that the line was leased to the North Eastern Railway which started a regular, but short-lived, passenger service from that date.

Brigham – Bullgill

Passenger service withdrawn	29 April 1935		*Stations closed*	*Date*
Distance	5.5 miles		Dovenby (private station)	probably 29 April 1935
Company	Maryport & Carlisle Railway		Linefoot	1 November 1908
			Papcastle *	1 July 1921
Stations closed	*Date*			
Dearham	29 April 1935			

* Remained open for quarrymen's traffic, but was finally closed after May 1922.

Dearham Station, looking north.

Promoted by a small local company to extend its territory towards Cockermouth, this line opened on 12 April 1867 with a west-facing junction on the Cockermouth & Workington Railway. It provided a new route for iron ore traffic northwards from Cleator towards Carlisle. The M&CR gained running powers over the Cockermouth & Workington line eastwards into Cockermouth, thus Maryport to Cockermouth trains had to reverse at both Bullgill and Brigham. In later years a through service between Keswick and Carlisle was worked over this route. From 24 March 1887 Linefoot was a junction with the Northern Extension of the Cleator & Workington Junction Railway and became an exchange point for coke traffic from the North-East.

Calva Junction – Linefoot Junction

Passenger service withdrawn   Calva Junction – Seaton: February 1922; Seaton – Linefoot: November 1908

Distance   5.25 miles

Company   Cleator & Workington Junction Railway

Stations closed	*Date*
Seaton	February 1922
Great Broughton	November 1908

Seaton Station in the 1930s with two generations of signal box flanking the station building.

The Northern Extension of the C&WJR was the result of an attempt by this small local company to take a greater share, in terms of distance hauled, of the coke traffic from the North-East. Originally intended as a route to totally bypass both the LNWR and M&CR lines by projecting the line as far as the Solway Junction line north of Brayton, the recession of the 1880s led to a more prudent vision and the line was terminated at a junction with the M&CR at Linefoot. Passenger services over the section between Seaton and Linefoot were very short lived, having started only on 1 September 1908. Services to Seaton were primarily for workmen, running through to the colliery at Lowca on the Lowca Light Railway. The through link to Linefoot became redundant with wartime rationalisation, closing totally from 1 September 1921. However, much of the line survived until 4 June 1992, first to serve Buckhill Colliery (closed in 1932) and later as a connection to the military arms depot at Broughton Moor (see also pages 31–32).

Carlisle (Port Carlisle Branch Junction) – Edinburgh (Portobello East Junction)

Passenger service withdrawn	6 January 1969
Distance	Port Carlisle Junction – Scottish border at Kershopefoot: 20.5 miles
Company	North British Railway

Stations closed	Date
Port Carlisle Junction	1 July 1864
Parkhouse Halt *	6 January 1969

Stations closed	Date
Harker **	1 November 1929
Lyneside	5 June 1950
Longtown	6 January 1969
Scotch Dyke	2 May 1949
Riddings Junction	15 June 1964
Penton	6 January 1969
Kershopefoot	6 January 1969

Longtown Station. The signals controlled the junction for the branch to Gretna (see page 23).

* This station did not appear on public timetables.

** Later reopened for workmen's services and finally closed from 6 January 1969.

The North British Railway had extended its system southwards from Edinburgh to Hawick as early as 1849, although even then this was seen as the first section of a route to Carlisle where the company intended to compete with the Caledonian Railway for the lucrative Edinburgh traffic from the West Coast main line. The Caledonian was equally determined to keep its competitor out. Despite the bleak rugged country which separated the towns of the Tweed Valley from the Solway Plain, a whole series of competing proposals were put forward by both companies. It was 1859 before the North British won powers for the Border Union Railway from Hawick into Carlisle, where the company took over the ailing Carlisle & Silloth Bay Railway for the opening of its new line on 1 July 1862. From the opening of the Settle and Carlisle line by the Midland Railway on 1 May 1876 the North British entered into a partnership by which the Waverley line became part of a third Anglo–Scottish trunk route, a status which it enjoyed well into the British Rail period. 'The Waverley' express between London St Pancras and Edinburgh Waverley finally ceased to run in the mid-1960s, but the final demise of the line itself came as a result of the Beeching Report of 1963.

Clapham – Low Gill

Passenger service withdrawn	1 February 1954	*Stations closed*	*Date*
Distance	County boundary at Kirkby Lonsdale –	Barbon *	1 February 1954
	Low Gill: 13.75 miles	Middleton	13 April 1931
Company	London & North Western Railway	Sedbergh *	1 February 1954

Middleton Station was known as Middleton-on-Lune until 19 July 1926.

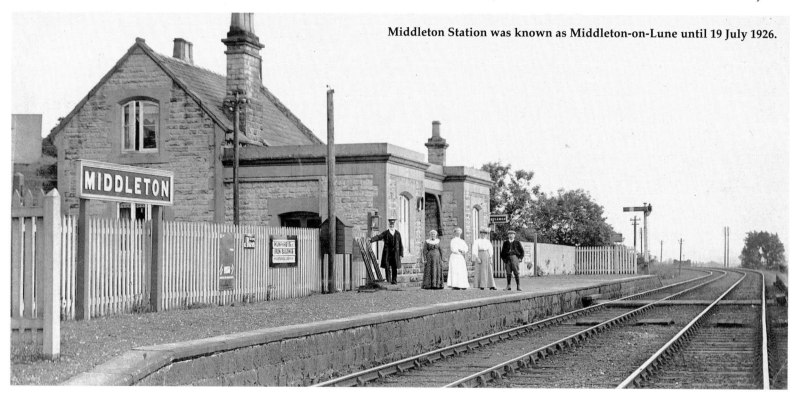

A branch line which should have been a through route is one way this line was once described. Under pressure from the LNWR, it was promoted by the Lancaster & Carlisle Railway in a complex game of strategy played out against the Midland Railway in the 1850s to block that company's moves to gain a route to Scotland over the L&C after the takeover by the Midland of the North Western Railway and its line from Skipton to Morecambe. The LNWR had obtained powers for its own line from Clapham to join the L&C in the Lune Valley, but these were abandoned for the section north of Ingleton because of shortage of funds before the Midland took over. The line opened for passengers to an end-on junction with the Midland, just north of Ingleton, on 16 September 1861.

* Remained open for term-end scholars' (from two local public schools) traffic to Sedbergh and Barbon.

Sedbergh Station.

After opening the LNWR took all possible steps to discourage through traffic from the Midland, passengers having to transfer between two stations at Ingleton which were separated by a viaduct. The obstructive tactics to any development of through Scottish traffic by this route was one of the factors which led the Midland to put forward proposals for its own route to the north – the Settle and Carlisle line. Train services on this line were never more than those of a remote rural branch, but at one time they did include a through service between Kendal and Ingleton. After closure of local passenger services the line continued to carry local goods traffic until local goods stations closed from 1 October 1964. It was also an important diversionary route, last performing this function during the snow blockage of the Settle and Carlisle line in the winter of 1963. It finally closed to all traffic in 1967.

Conishead Priory – Plumpton Junction

Passenger service withdrawn	1 January 1917	*Stations closed*	*Date*
Distance	2 miles	North Lonsdale Ironworks Halt *	Unknown
Company	Furness Railway	Conishead Priory	1 January 1917

* This station did not appear on public timetables.

In its period of maximum prosperity in the late 1870s the Furness Railway conceived a plan to build a new main line from Plumpton Junction, east of Ulverston, to Barrow, in order to avoid the steep climb to Lindal Summit and the problems caused in that area by subsidence from the extensive iron ore mining. The scheme failed to materialise and the line terminated at Conishead Priory, although it also served the North Lonsdale Ironworks. A daily service of two mixed trains started from 27 June 1883, later reduced to just one. Beyond the ironworks the line closed in a round of wartime economies, although the ironworks, and later the Glaxo chemical works on the same site, continued to be served by rail. While traffic to the chemical works had ceased in the early 1990s, this part of the line was only finally lifted in 2000.

Coniston – Foxfield

Passenger service withdrawn	6 October 1958	*Stations closed*	*Date*
Distance	10 miles	Broughton (first station)	1 June 1859
Company	Furness Railway	Broughton-in-Furness	6 October 1958
		Woodland	6 October 1958
		Torver	6 October 1958
		Coniston	6 October 1958

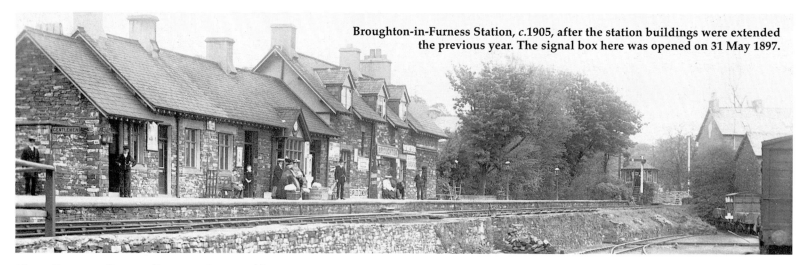

Broughton-in-Furness Station, c.1905, after the station buildings were extended the previous year. The signal box here was opened on 31 May 1897.

Woodland Station.

Copper mining around Coniston was the principal projected source of traffic for the Coniston Railway when it was promoted in 1857 by a company that was closely linked to the Furness Railway which put up nearly one quarter of the necessary capital. The line was opened on 18 June 1859 from Broughton which at that time was the northern terminus of the Furness Railway. Copper mining was soon to decline, however, and the Furness Railway turned to tourism for the future of the line. To this end the company operated two steam yachts on Coniston Water. One of them, 'Gondola', was launched as early as October 1859 and is still sailing today after substantial reconstruction in the 1970s. It is now owned by the National Trust.

Coniston Station in the 1930s. Final closure to all traffic came on 30 April 1962.

Distington – Parton

Passenger service withdrawn	1 September 1914	*Stations closed*	*Date*
Distance	3 miles	Parton Halt *	1 April 1929
Company	London & North Western and Furness Joint Railway		

* This station did not appear on public timetables.

Promoted as a last gesture by the Whitehaven Cleator & Egremont Railway before its joint takeover by the two neighbouring railway companies, who subsequently completed it, this single track branch ran from a junction on the Marron extension of the WC&E to the Whitehaven Junction line of the LNWR at Parton, running through the new ironworks at Distington and serving various collieries en route. The line opened on 23 October 1879 and a short-lived passenger service between Distington and Whitehaven started on 1 June 1881, ending on 8 December 1883. Passenger services were reintroduced on this section from 1 October 1913, ceasing again exactly eleven months later. Yet another service ran for workmen, but only to the new Parton Halt from 11 January 1915 to 1 April 1929. Total closure east of Distington took place on 14 February 1929, and between Distington and Bain's Pit Siding on 2 May 1932. This last stub, serving the colliery and other industries at Lowca, survived until 23 May 1973.

Gretna – Longtown

Passenger service withdrawn	9 August 1915	*Station closed*	*Date*
Distance	3.25 miles	Gretna (NBR)	9 August 1915
Company	North British Railway		

The NBR station at Gretna.

Branching off the Border Union Railway at Longtown (see page 16) was a branch to Gretna, with a connection onto the Caledonian main line just south of Gretna Junction Station. Between the two junctions at Gretna, of the Caledonian with the North British and with the Glasgow & South Western Railway, the NBR had running powers over 24 chains of line and along this a service was operated between Longtown and Gretna Green (G&SWR), the only one of three Gretna stations actually in Scotland. The NBR had its own terminus station, just a few yards to the east of the Caledonian station, and NBR trains called at all three stations in both directions! With the construction of the new Kingmoor Marshalling Yard north of Carlisle in the early 1960s, the branch was converted into an up goods line to take traffic from the Waverley line onto the former Caledonian line to enter the yard from the north, and a new southwards facing junction was made at Mossband. After closure of the Waverley line in 1969 the west end of the branch was retained as a siding to serve the Ammunition Depot. From 1915 a vast munitions factory was built alongside the branch which reached far over the Scottish border beyond Gretna and to which the branch provided access, a function which continues to this day. The factory had its own extensive railway system upon which internal passenger services were operated and this is covered in *Dumfries and Galloway's Lost Railways*.

Kirkby Stephen East – Tebay

Passenger service withdrawn	1 December 1952	*Stations closed*	*Date*
Distance	11.25 miles	Ravenstonedale	1 December 1952
Company	North Eastern Railway	Gaisgill	1 December 1952

LMS-designed 2-6-0, No. 46472, leaves Ravenstonedale Station with a train for Kirkby Stephen.

Encouraged by the rapid rise of the iron smelting industry of the Furness area, which was remote from supplies of coal and coke, landowners and others promoted the South Durham & Lancashire Union Railway to link the Furness area across the Pennines with the Durham coalfield at Barnard Castle. Starting from Tebay on the Lancaster & Carlisle Railway, and opening on 4 July 1861 for mineral traffic (five weeks later for passengers), the line was dramatically engineered over the 1,370 foot high Stainmore Summit by Thomas Bouch with many spectacular viaducts, much of them now demolished. Daily passenger services between Tebay and Kirkby Stephen were withdrawn ten years before total closure, which came with the ending of coke traffic to the Barrow Iron & Steel Works and diversion of the remaining traffic to Millom Ironworks via Carlisle. This final closure, from 22 January 1962, also brought an end to the summer Saturday only service between Newcastle and Blackpool which traversed this section of line (see pages 10–12).

Lakeside – Plumpton Junction/Leven Junction

Passenger service withdrawn	26 September 1938 *	*Stations closed*	*Date*
Distance	7.75 miles	Lakeside	6 September 1965
Company	Furness Railway	Newby Bridge Halt **	12 September 1939
		Haverthwaite ***	30 September 1946
		Greenodd ****	30 September 1946

Lakeside Station. Empty stock from excursion trains is stabled in the station and yard.

* This date marked the end of year round services. The summer service continued until 31 August 1941. Reopened for seasonal services only from 3 June 1946, closing on 6 September 1965. Reopened again for seasonal services between Lakeside and Haverthwaite by the Lakeside & Haverthwaite Railway from 2 May 1973.

** Closed temporarily for a short period after 1 January 1917. Reopened by L&HR from 2 May 1973.
*** Previously closed from 16 September 1940 to 3 June 1946. Reopened by L&HR from 2 May 1973.
**** Previously closed from 16 September 1940 to 3 June 1946.

The Furness Railway promoted its branch to the southern end of Windermere at Newby Bridge in 1866, the line being completed on 23 April 1869. By that time, however, it had already been decided that more capacious accommodation for both trains and steamers was necessary and powers were obtained to extend the line to a new quay at Windermere Lakeside, opening on 1 June of the same year. The Act for the branch also empowered the Furness Railway to buy the Windermere United Steam Yacht Company which had been operating on the lake since the 1840s, effectively extending the Furness company into the heart of the Lake District at Ambleside. The branch and the steamers were to become vital components in the Furness Railway's very active promotion of tourism in southern Lakeland in its attempts to compensate for the seriously declining industrial traffic from the 1880s. A series of new steamers were built by the company, joined by two further ones built by the London Midland & Scottish Railway in the 1930s. These were all moved by rail in sections and assembled on the slipway at Lakeside. The east facing curve to Leven Junction on the Furness Railway main line, built to accommodate through excursion traffic from Lancashire and Yorkshire, closed in 1952.

Lowca – Harrington Junction

Passenger service withdrawn	31 May 1926		
Distance	3.5 miles		
Company	Lowca Light Railway/		
	Cleator & Workington Junction Railway		

Stations closed	*Date*
Lowca (LLR) *	31 May 1926

Stations closed	*Date*
Micklam (LLR) *	31 May 1926
Copperas Hill (LLR)	June 1921
Rosehill (Archer Street) Halt (C&WJR) *	31 May 1926
Harrington Church Road (C&WJR) *	31 May 1926

* Remained open for workmen's services until 1 April 1929.

A Workington Iron & Steel Co. 0-6-0ST surmounts the 1 in 7 climb from Rosehill Junction into Copperas Hill Station.

An ancient wagonway had connected a series of small collieries south of Harrington with the harbour there since the eighteenth century, later becoming a mineral railway owned from 1909 by the Workington Iron & Steel Company. In 1913 a Light Railway Order was obtained to operate workers' trains over the branch connection with the C&WJR from Harrington Junction to Rosehill. While most trains ran from Workington Central, one a day ran through from Seaton. They were worked by Furness Railway locomotives and rolling stock. The service commenced on 2 June 1913 and trains had to climb the formidable 1 in 17 gradient up Copperas Hill from a standing start at Archer Street – the steepest adhesion-worked gradient in Britain over which regular passenger trains ran. After closure to passengers the line continued to be worked by the steel company for internal traffic between its plants and finally closed from 27 May 1973.

Marron Junction West – Moor Row

Passenger service withdrawn	13 April 1931		*Stations closed*	*Date*
Distance	14 miles		Winder *	13 April 1931
Company	London & North Western		Yeathouse **	13 April 1931
	and Furness Joint Railway		Eskett	2 August 1875
			Frizington *	13 April 1931
			Cleator Moor (first station)	19 April 1866
Stations closed	*Date*		Cleator Moor East *	13 April 1931
Bridgefoot	13 April 1931			
Branthwaite	13 April 1931		* Reopened to workmen's services from 11 March 1940 to 8 April 1940.	
Ullock	13 April 1931		** Replaced Eskett.	
Lamplugh	13 April 1931			
Rowrah	13 April 1931			

The rich hematite iron ore field around Cleator attracted the interest of local railway promoters in the early 1850s. Like all the lines centred on Whitehaven at this time it was strongly backed by the Earl of Lonsdale and opened from Mirehouse Junction, about one mile south of Corkickle, to Moor Row, diverging there with a northwards branch to Frizington. It opened to passenger traffic from 1 July 1857, some eighteen months after mineral traffic on the line had started. Extremely prosperous from the start, the line was extended in stages down the Marron Valley to a triangular junction with the Cockermouth & Workington Railway. This was reached by passenger services from 2 April 1866. This extension provided an alternative route between the ore field and the growing number of iron furnaces around Workington, avoiding the congested coastal route, with the single bore Bransty tunnel, through Whitehaven. In following years the line sprouted many short branches and diversions to reach new iron mines and to

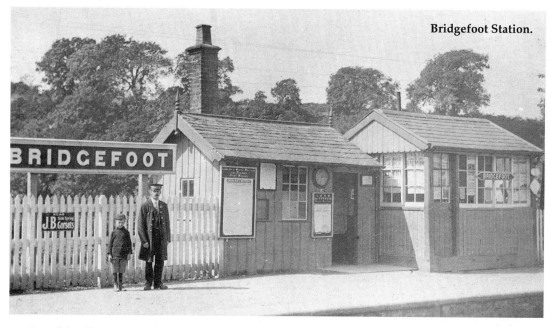

Bridgefoot Station.

avoid areas of mining subsidence. After the promotion of the Cleator & Workington Junction Railway in the mid-1870s the directors of the Whitehaven, Cleator & Egremont Railway at last succumbed to approaches from the LNW and Furness Railways and agreed to a joint takeover which became effective from 1 July 1879. Passenger services were an early casualty of bus competition and by that time the ore field was approaching exhaustion. A long process of decline saw the line from Corkickle to Rowrah survive for mineral traffic into the 1970s (see also pages 38–39).

Mealsgate – Aspatria

			Stations closed	Date
Passenger service withdrawn	22 September 1930		Mealsgate	22 September 1930
Distance	4.25 miles		Allhallows Colliery *	probably during 1928
Company	Maryport & Carlisle Railway		Baggrow	22 September 1930

A Maryport & Carlisle Railway 0-6-0 at Mealsgate Station, *c*.1900.

Built in response to a proposed line, backed by the North British Railway, to tap traffic from the north-eastern arm of the West Cumberland coalfield, this branch opened on 26 December 1866 to serve a number of collieries, all of which had closed by 1928. The line hung on for local goods traffic until final closure from 1 December 1952.

* This station did not appear on public timetables.

Mealsgate – Aikbank Junction

Passenger service withdrawn	1 August 1921	*Station closed*	*Date*
Distance	3 miles	High Blaithwaite	1 August 1921
Company	Maryport & Carlisle Railway		

High Blaithwaite Station. In 1910 this tiny station only saw two or three trains a day.

A short continuation of the Mealsgate branch looped back into the Maryport & Carlisle main line to provide a through link with Wigton. This section was never continuously open to traffic and was not used between 1869 and 1877. The single station was only one short carriage length and, with the branch itself, became the victim of an early operating economy.

Moor Row (Cleator Moor Junction) – Siddick Junction

Passenger service withdrawn	13 April 1931		*Stations closed*	*Date*
Distance	11.25 miles		Moresby Parks	13 April 1931
Company	Cleator & Workington Junction Railway		Millgrove (private station) *	*c.*1921
			Distington	13 April 1931
			High Harrington	13 April 1931
Stations closed	*Date*		Workington Central	13 April 1931
Cleator Moor West	13 April 1931			
Keekle Colliers' Platform *	1 October 1923		* These did not appear on public timetables.	
Moresby Junction	1 October 1923			

**A Furness railway 0-6-0 heads away from High Harrington Station
with a train for Siddick.**

Workington Central Station pictured sometime after the closure of passenger services in 1931.

After the locally promoted and built networks of railways in West Cumberland had succumbed in their prosperity to takeovers by the LNWR and the Furness Railway, the principal customers, the ironmasters of Workington and the iron ore proprietors around Cleator, became so irritated by high costs and poor service that they determined to promote their own line linking the Cleator ore field with the Workington iron furnaces. So the Cleator & Workington Junction Railway – 'the track of the ironmasters' – was formed and subsequently opened to passengers between Moor Row and Workington from 1 October 1879, extending to the junction with the LNWR at Siddick exactly eleven months later. By agreement with the Furness Railway, that company operated all main line trains, both passenger and heavy mineral traffic, over the C&WJR until grouping in 1923. Most branch traffic was handled by the C&WJR's own small fleet of locomotives (for other sections of the C&WJR, see also pages 8, 15 and 27).

Penrith (Keswick Junction) – Workington (Derwent Junction)

Passenger service withdrawn   Workington –
Keswick: 18 April 1966
Keswick – Penrith: 6 March 1972

Distance   40 miles
Company   London & North Western Railway /
Cockermouth, Keswick & Penrith Railway

Stations closed	*Date*
Blencow *	6 March 1972
Penruddock	6 March 1972
Troutbeck	6 March 1972
Highgate Platform **	December 1928
Threlkeld	6 March 1972

Stations closed	*Date*
Briery Halt **	17 November 1958
Keswick	6 March 1972
Braithwaite	18 April 1966
Bassenthwaite Lake	18 April 1966
Embleton	15 September 1958
Cockermouth (first station)	2 January 1865
Cockermouth ***	18 April 1966
Brigham	18 April 1966
Broughton Cross	2 March 1942
Marron Junction (transfer platform only)	1 July 1897
Camerton ****	3 March 1952
Workington Bridge	1 January 1951

* Previously closed on 3 March 1952; reopened on 2 July 1956.
** These stations did not appear on public timetables.
*** A joint station run by the CK&PR, LNWR and M&CR.
**** Remained open for workmen's services.

Penruddock Station, looking towards Penrith.

Ex-LNWR 0-6-0, No. 58389, leaving Threlkeld Station for Penrith, *c*.1950.

The first section of this route across the northern Lake District, the Cockermouth & Workington Railway, opened on 28 April 1847, connecting the main market town of West Cumberland to the developing rail network along the coast while also opening up new markets for the growing collieries of the lower Derwent Valley by linking them direct to the port of Workington. From 1865, with the opening of the Cockermouth Keswick & Penrith Railway, it became part of the railway route across the northern Lake District.

A LNWR 'DX' 0-6-0 approaching Keswick Station with a train from Workington, *c*.1900.

The Cockermouth, Keswick & Penrith Railway was promoted as the final link in a route between South Durham and West Cumberland primarily for use in the transport of coke westwards and iron ore in the opposite direction. It also opened up the potential for tourist traffic to the northern Lake District. Strongly supported by both the LNW and North Eastern Railways, the line was engineered by Thomas Bouch and opened for passengers on 2 January 1865, mineral trains already having been in operation since 26 October the previous year. The quantity of coke traffic necessitated the doubling of nine and a half miles of the route east of Keswick in the 1890s, but by 1914 much of the coke traffic had gone with the building of a new generation of coke ovens in West Cumberland.

Staff and passengers pose at Brigham Station as an M&CR 2-4-0, probably No. R1, awaits departure for Cockermouth.

The CK&P company had no locomotives or rolling stock of its own and had entered into working agreements with the LNW and NE Railways, the former handling passenger and local goods traffic, and the latter the through mineral workings. Passenger trains therefore were usually worked through from Workington over the Cockermouth & Workington line (see above). Between the wars the line was actively promoted for tourism by the LMS, and in summer carried its own named train 'The Lakes Express' from Euston. But despite a post-war tourist boom and the early introduction of diesel units from 3 January 1955 the line became a victim of the Beeching cuts of the mid-1960s, when the western end through to Workington was closed, the eastern end following six years later.

Piel – Barrow (Salthouse Junction)

Passenger service withdrawn	6 July 1936	*Stations closed*	*Date*
Distance	3 miles	Piel	6 July 1936
Company	Furness Railway	Rampside	6 July 1936
		Salthouse Halt Platform	before 1936

Rampside Station with Furness Railway 2-4-0, No. 4, running in from Barrow.

Most of this short branch had been part of the original route of the Furness Railway, opened from 24 August 1846, when trains linked with steamer services from Fleetwood across Morecambe Bay. With the destruction of the pier at Piel by a great storm in 1852, and the rapid development of Barrow, the line became a backwater. From 1867 new steamer services to the Isle of Man and Belfast revived the branch for a while until the new pier in Walney Channel (Ramsden Dock Station) was opened in 1881. From 1873 a new curve linked the branch directly to Barrow via Salthouse Junction where a halt was opened for workers at the nearby paper mill.

Sellafield – Corkickle via Moor Row

Passenger service withdrawn	7 January 1935	*Stations closed*	*Date*
Distance	10.25 miles	Woodend *	7 January 1935
Company	London & North Western	Egremont *	7 January 1935
	and Furness Joint Railway	St Thomas Cross Platform **	by June 1952
		Beckermet Mines **	Unknown
Stations closed	*Date*	Beckermet *	7 January 1935
Moor Row *	7 January 1935		

Moor Row Station and junction, *c.*1950. The line to Egremont curves right behind the signal box.

* The line and these stations were temporarily reopened between 6 May 1946 and 16 June 1947. Workmen's services between Sellafield and Moor Row continued until 6 September 1965, and a scholars' service from Seascale to Egremont operated from September 1964 to 11 December 1969.

** These stations did not appear on public timetables.

Beckermet Station, *c*.1917.

The other line from Moor Row which opened as an original part of the Whitehaven, Cleator & Egremont Railway diverged southwards to Egremont. This was also extended to avoid the congestion around Whitehaven, as large quantities of iron ore were sent by rail from around Cleator to the Barrow area for smelting. Opposition to this proposal from the Whitehaven & Furness Junction Railway, which up to now carried this traffic, was eventually resolved by agreement to build the new line jointly as the Cleator & Furness Railway, but worked by the WC&ER. The line opened on 2 August 1869. Again further branches were built to serve nearby iron mines and quarries, the last of these to Beckermet Mines closing with the remaining sections of the former WC&E to Whitehaven via Moor Row from 1 November 1980. The section between Beckermet Mines Junction and Sellafield closed to all traffic from 19 January 1970 (see also page 28).

Silloth/Port Carlisle – Carlisle (Canal Junction):

Port Carlisle – Drumburgh

Passenger service withdrawn	1 June 1932 *	*Stations closed*	*Date*
Distance	2.5 miles	Port Carlisle	1 June 1932
Company	North British Railway	Glasson	1 June 1932

Preparing the line at Port Carlisle for the reintroduction of locomotive-hauled trains, 6 April 1914. The horse tram beyond is now preserved in the National Railway Museum.

The horse tram at Port Carlisle Station, 23 September 1912.

* The line was previously closed from 1 January 1917 to 1 February 1919.

Silloth/Port Carlisle – Carlisle (Canal Junction):

Silloth – Carlisle (Canal Junction)

Passenger service withdrawn	7 September 1964
Distance	20.5 miles
Company	North British Railway

Station closed	*Date*
Silloth	7 September 1964
Silloth Convalescent Home *	Unknown
Blackdyke Halt	7 September 1964
Abbey Town	7 September 1964

Stations closed	*Date*
Abbey Junction	1 September 1921
Kirkbride	7 September 1964
Drumburgh	4 July 1955
Burgh-by-Sands	7 September 1964
Kirkandrews	7 September 1964
Carlisle Canal	1 July 1864

* This station did not appear on public timetables.

Silloth Station, showing the extensive track layout which served the docks and the corn mill.

Villagers waiting at Burgh-by-Sands Station for the train to the market at Carlisle.

The Carlisle – Port Carlisle line originated from the conversion of the Carlisle Canal to a railway and opened to passengers on 22 June 1854. However, at the same time an extension was being promoted to a new port at Silloth on the Solway coast and this opened from Drumburgh on 28 August 1856. The heavy investment in the new dock and town soon proved beyond the financial resources of the small local company and the two lines were taken into the hands of the North British Railway on completion of its line from Hawick to Carlisle in 1862. The main claim to fame of the Port Carlisle line was that after the Silloth extension was completed the company decided to operate passenger services from Drumburgh with a horse-drawn 'dandy' car. This practice lasted until the line was rebuilt for locomotive haulage and horse operation ended on 4 April 1914. Silloth provided the NBR with access to the Irish Sea trade via its new port and also became a popular resort for the Scottish market. The railway succumbed to the Beeching rationalisations, but the port continues to be active without its rail connection.

Closed passenger stations on lines still open to passenger services

Line/service   **Carlisle – Whitehaven – Barrow – Carnforth**
(Maryport & Carlisle Railway: Carlisle – Maryport;
London & North Western Railway: Maryport
Junction – Whitehaven [Bransty]; Furness Railway:
Whitehaven [Bransty] – Carnforth)

Stations closed	Date
Carlisle Crown Street	17 March 1849
Bogfield	30 December 1844
Cummersdale *	18 June 1951
Crofton (private station) **	27 March 1954

Stations closed	Date
Curthwaite	12 June 1950
Micklethwaite	June 1845
Brookfield	10 February 1845
Heathfield	2 February 1848
Leegate	5 June 1950
Low Row	2 February 1848
Brayton	5 June 1950
Warthole Sidings **	Unknown
Bullgill	7 March 1960
Dearham Bridge	5 June 1950

A LNWR 'Cauliflower' 0-6-0 at Siddick Junction Station, shunting traffic from St Helen's No. 3 Colliery.

* Workmen's trains continued to stop here after this date.   ** These did not appear on public timetables.

Line/service	**Carlisle – Whitehaven – Barrow – Carnforth**	Stations closed	Date
	(continued)	Monk Moors **	9 June 1958
		Whitbeck Crossing	September 1857
Stations closed	Date	Kirksanton Crossing	September 1857
Maryport (first station)	4 June 1860	Under Hill	December 1859
St Helen's Halt *	Unknown	Barrow Rabbit Hill (first station)	c.October 1862
Siddick Junction	1 October 1934	Barrow Strand (second station)	1 June 1882
Whitehaven (first station)	24 December 1874	Furness Abbey	25 September 1950
Whitehaven Newtown	30 September 1852	Lindal	1 October 1951
St Bees Golf Halt *	February 1918	Wraysholme Halt *	Unknown
Eskmeals	3 August 1959	Meathop Halt *	Unknown

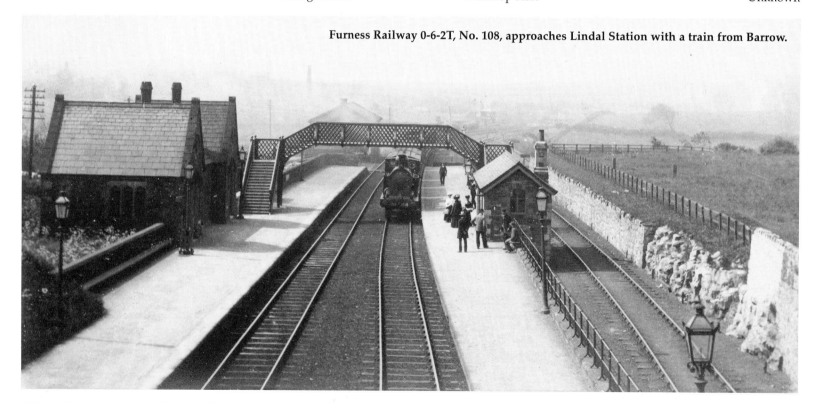

Furness Railway 0-6-2T, No. 108, approaches Lindal Station with a train from Barrow.

* These did not appear on public timetables.   ** Opened in 1897 and closed c.1920. Reopened in 1940. This also did not appear on public timetables.

Line/service	Carlisle – Carnforth – London Euston
	(London & North Western Railway)

Stations closed	Date
Brisco	December 1852
Wreay	16 August 1943
Southwaite	7 April 1952
Calthwaite	7 April 1952
Plumpton	31 May 1948
Clifton & Lowther	4 July 1938
Shap	1 July 1968

Stations closed	Date
Shap Quarry *	Unknown
Tebay	1 July 1968
Low Gill	7 March 1960
Low Gill (first station)	16 September 1861
Grayrigg	1 February 1954
Grayrigg Halt	1 November 1849
Milnthorpe	1 July 1968
Burton & Holme	27 March 1950

* This station did not appear on public timetables.

A train of LNWR six-wheel carriages, bound for Keswick from Carlisle, at Southwaite Station.

Burton & Holme was a typical local station on the Lancaster & Carlisle line.

Ex-LNWR 4-4-2T, No. 6784, leaves Tebay Station with a southbound local train.

Line/service	Carlisle – Settle Junction – Leeds	
	(Midland Railway)	

Stations closed	Date
Scotby	1 February 1942
Cumwhinton	5 November 1956
Cotehill	7 April 1952
Armathwaite *	4 May 1970
Lazonby & Kirkoswald *	4 May 1970
Little Salkeld	4 May 1970

Stations closed	Date
Langwathby *	4 May 1970
Culgaith	4 May 1970
New Biggin	4 May 1970
Long Marton	4 May 1970
Ormside	2 June 1952
Crosby Garrett	6 October 1952
Kirkby Stephen *	4 May 1970
Garsdale *	4 May 1970
Dent *	4 May 1970

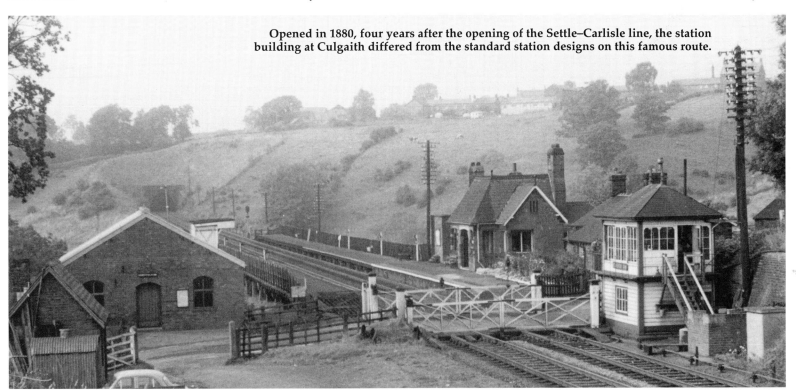

Opened in 1880, four years after the opening of the Settle–Carlisle line, the station building at Culgaith differed from the standard station designs on this famous route.

* These stations were reopened from 14 July 1986. Those previously reopened from 3 May 1975 for occasional 'Dalesrail' services were Dent, Garsdale and Kirkby Stephen. Langwathby, Lazonby and Armathwaite were reopened for these services from a later date.

Line/service **Carlisle – Newcastle** (North Eastern Railway)

Stations closed	*Date*
Carlisle (London Road)	1 January 1863
Scotby	2 November 1959
Wetheral *	2 January 1967
Heads Nook	2 January 1967

Stations closed	*Date*
How Mill	5 January 1959
Naworth	5 May 1952
Low Row	5 January 1959

* Reopened from 5 October 1981.

The position of the signalbox at Wetheral Station, high on the bank, gave it visibility round the sharp curve.